Louise Ivory Moore

Diamonds in History and Romance

Louise Ivory Moore

Diamonds in History and Romance

ISBN/EAN: 9783337050900

Printed in Europe, USA, Canada, Australia, Japan

Cover: Foto ©ninafisch / pixelio.de

More available books at **www.hansebooks.com**

Diamonds
In History and Romance

By Louise Ivory Moore

Chicago
The Schulte Publishing Company
323-325 Dearborn Street

Copyright A. D. MDCCCXCVII
By Francis J. Schulte

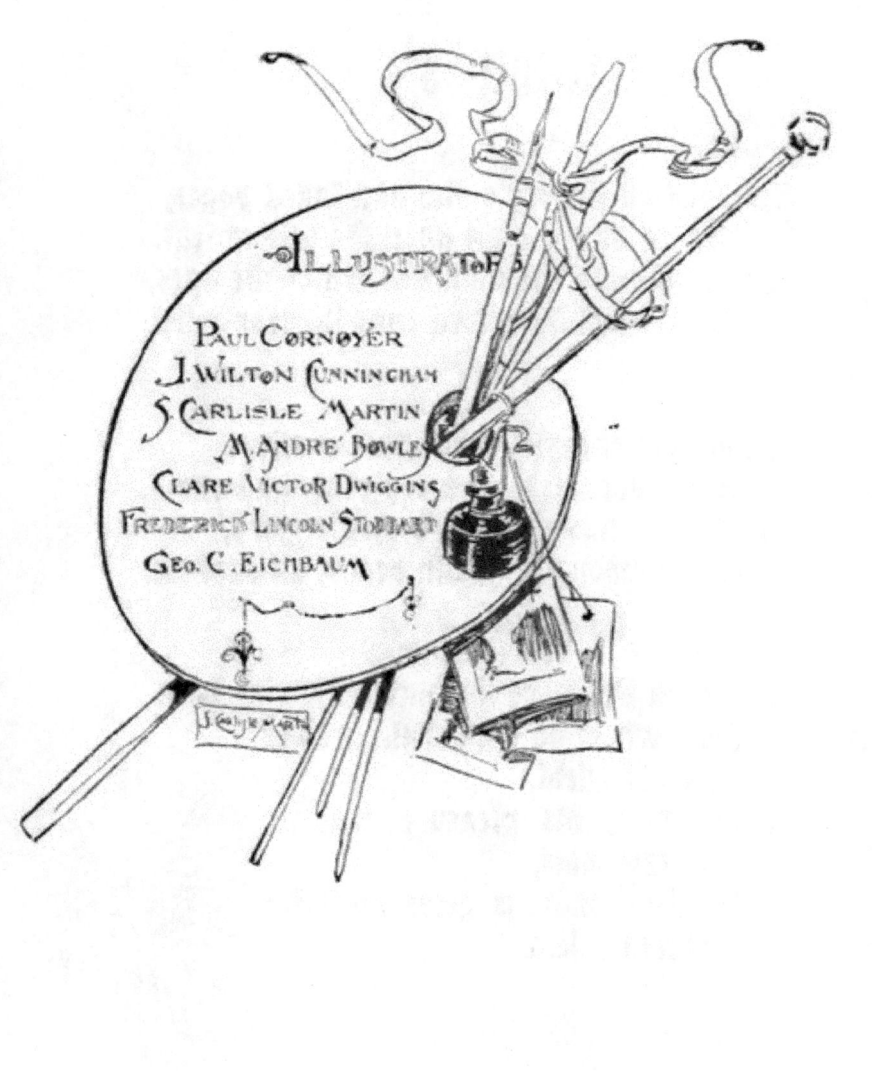

Diamonds

Far back on History's dim and faded pages,
  Traced by the quill upon the vellum leaf,
Down through the countless era of the ages,
  The Diamond's record runs in clear relief.

In ancient chronicle and modern story,
  A radiant queen in every court and clime,
Within its crystal walls a magic glory,
  The Diamond reigns in beauty all sublime.

The High Priest of the ancient Jewish host,
  Than whom no man could greater power wield,
Bore, when his pleasure was to dazzle most,
  Twelve wondrous gems upon his sacred shield.

To
The American Woman:
A Princess in her own right,
And, in every land she seeks,
The gem-crowned Queen
of
Love and Beauty

M. ANDRE BOWLES.

"Far back on History's dim and faded pages,
Traced by the quill upon the vellum leaf."

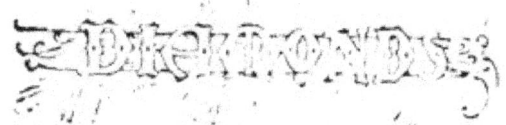

Twelve wondrous gems: and which amongst them all
   Dare vie in beauty or in sparkling light
With Jahalom? For so did Hebrews call
   That which to-day we know as Diamond bright.

When centuries, alternate peace and strife,
   Had passed away, and Roman might and power
Bowed 'neath its yoke the stream of human life
   As blustering north wind bends the swaying flower,

Imperial matrons, with their bright, dark eyes,
   Fashioned their classic robes of cloth-of-gold,
And woven purple plunged in Tyrian dyes,
   And clasped a precious jewel in each fold.

Those glittering gems were sometimes tro-
  phies rare,
    Snatched from their victims of a van-
      quished race,
Their value often far beyond compare,
    Yet none too splendid for patrician grace.

Wife of Caligula, Rome's tyrant Lord,
    Lollia Paulina,—Pliny tells the story,—
Presided at a gorgeous nuptial board,
    In pearls and diamonds, a blaze of glory.

Twined in the meshes of her raven hair,
    On dimpled arms as alabaster white,
'Round swan-like neck and slender fingers
  fair,
    Myriads of jewels shed their luster bright.

Two million pieces all of shining gold,
　　The bribes of princes, from her grandsire's hoard,
To gain the favor of the Emperor's friend,
　　Had for this wealth of jewels been outpoured.

But in those days of old imperial Rome
　　Most rare and precious was the queen of gems,
And seldom were its flashing colors shown
　　Save in the royal rings or diadems.

For only on far India's distant shore
　　The dusky natives, in the pebbled stream
Or rocky mine, while seeking golden ore,
　　Found guerdon rich the Diamond's longed-for gleam.

Virtues most wondrous Plato it
    assigned.
Magnanimous in peace, in
    conflict bold,
Was he whose happy fortune
    't was to find
This ever precious "kernel in
    the gold."

The powdered dust that from its crushing fell
    Was deemed endowed with magic power
    beside
To avert the deadly flash of lightning's spell,
    With supernatural gift that none denied.

In history's epochs Diamonds played a part
    Not second even to Damascus blade:
To gain the spoil quick steel would seek the
    heart,
    And honor little in the balance weighed.

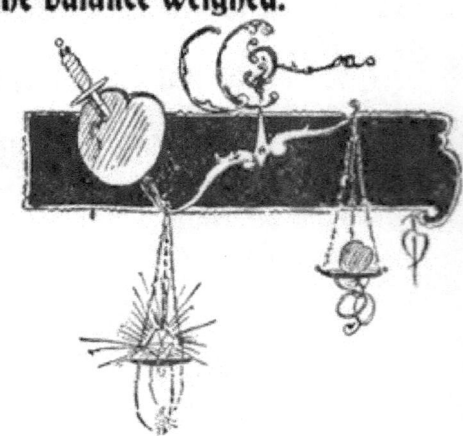

FREDERICK LINCOLN STODDARD.
"To gain the spoil, quick steel would seek the heart."

They gemmed the Peacock Throne of Nadir
   Shah,
   Gleamed in the jeweled hilt of Charles the
      Bold,
Purchased a crown for Ibrahim Pasha,
   And for their sake a king his subjects sold.

The snow-white plume of Henry of Navarre
   A diamond buckle held in its proud place.
The "Virgin Queen" of England wore a star
   Of Diamonds in her stately ruff of lace.

The "Orloff," once a Brahmin idol's eye
   From Buddhist temple stolen by recreant
      priest,
Where Russia's Czar wields his great scep-
   ter high,
   Resplendent gleams, at grand levee or feast.

DIAMONDS

The "Koh-i-noor," that back to Krischna dates,
  Whose cutting false, when Aurungzebe's gem,
Cost sad Hortensio Borgia his estates,
  Now shines in England's royal diadem.

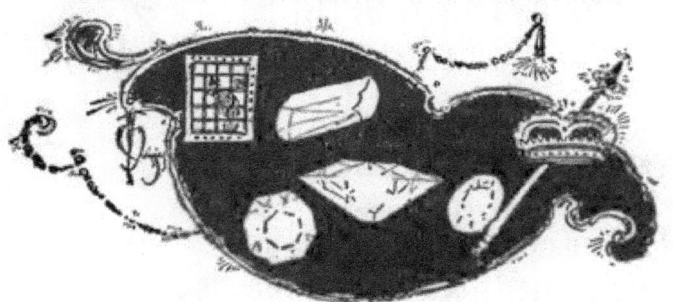

That noted jewel called the "Polar Star,"
  The "Regent," from the sword of Bonaparte,
"Mattam," "Braganza," "Cumberland," and "Shah,"
  Are names that lead the world's great diamond mart.

Nor always white. One Russian gem is red;
  The "Dresden Brilliant" of an emerald green;
A yellow tint the Tiffany's instead,
  And in the "Hope" a sapphire blue is seen.

The legend runs that once a faithful
    slave,
  A jeweled ring whilst carrying for
    his lord,
Beset by thieves, determined thus to save,
  Swallowed the gem before he met the
    sword.

Skilled surgeon's knife was needed to regain
  The diamond worth the ransom of a king.
The faithful servant had not died in vain:
  Back to his master's coffers went the ring.

One story stands, a blot that clouds the time:
  When diamonds were first found in Brazil,
The rulers of the sunny southern clime
  Measures enforced that worked the peo-
    ple's ill.

J. WILTON CUNNINGHAM.
"The stately damsels trod the minuet's maze."

DIAMONDS

Forth from their homes they drove the humble poor
   And seized their land, to delve for diamonds deep.
Razed to the ground, nor hearthstone they nor door,
   Were forced in woodland or in caves to sleep.

But Mother Nature's heart seemed touched at last.
   Brazil's supply decreased thro' fifty years,
And in their homes restored, their wanderings past,
   The poor in simple peace forgot their tears.

In our American Colonial days,
   With silken skirts, and powdered hair dressed high,
The stately damsels trod the minuet's maze,
   Their diamonds flashing as they glided by.

But when the Revolution's dread alarms
   Woke startled millions from their dream of peace,

The jewels were exchanged for warlike
   arms,
  To free our country and bid serfdom cease.

No gems were theirs, but
   sheen of golden hair,
  And teeth of pearl, thro'
   lips as rubies red.
Eyes diamond-bright lacked
   naught to make them
   fair: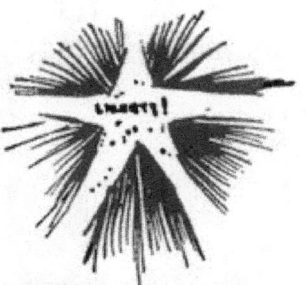
  The greatest jewel, Freedom, theirs instead.

Those patriotic times have fled fore'er.
  The merchant princes' daughters of to-day
The value of a petty kingdom wear,
  In baubles, at the opera or the play.

Crown diamonds, tokens of an empire's fall,
  Change hands, and cross the broad Atlan-
   tic's sweep,
To shine at plutocratic Gotham's ball
  While countless thousands cold and starv-
   ing weep.

DIAMONDS

Three decades since, where Afric' breasts the
    sea,
  A vast supply of diamonds was revealed;
Now 'neath the burning sky of Kimberly
  A myriad exiles eager seek the field.

Long days of toil go dragging hour by hour,
    Dread fevers lurk beneath the torrid sun,
The reptile's sting to fright has lost its power,
    While fortunes vast are daily sought and
    won.

In Borneo have also gems
    been found,
  And where the Ural Moun-
    tains raise their peaks;

PAUL CORNOYER.
"And Yuletide log, that warms the hearth and heart."

And for our own Virginia's fertile ground
  The "Oninoor," a monster brilliant, speaks.

Some have been mined where shines the Golden Gate;
  In Georgia's soil a few have come to light;
A wondrous stone came from the "Blue Grass State;"
  But Africa still leads the world in might.

The Diamond is Nature's miracle
  The carbon that is its component part
In bread we eat, in common coal does dwell,
  In Yuletide log that warms the hearth and heart.

DIAMONDS

But science proves volcanic fires, that boil
   With giant power, once did fiercely rage,
Forcing their way through rich magnesium
     soil,
   And wrought the Diamond in the Granite
     Age,

And crystallized its hues' prismatic glow,
   Like rainbow's arch, yet adamantine hard,
And pure as limpid streams that rippling flow
   Between the flowering banks of emerald
     sward.

Still, in the rough it only crystal seems;
   Pretty, and pleasing for a childish toy:
Beneath translucent surface hide the gleams
   That thrill the connoisseur with rapturous
     joy.

DIAMONDS

Not until lapidary's skill alone
   Has cut with labored toil the crust away
That veils with jealous walls of pebbled stone,
   The 'prisoned rainbow meets the light of day.

And oft unskillful workman will deface
   A priceless gem, for subtle is the art
Which shrewd Van Burghem early taught his race,
And clear-cut facets play a valued part.

So is the mind of man. Itself a prize,
   A gem far greater than earth else can yield;
But 't is on Education he relies
   To fit him for the senate or the field.

DIAMONDS

For, girt with opaque wall like Diamond stone,
  The untrained mind is like the pebbled
    sphere.
'T is learning's power can cut the crust alone,
  And Man stands forth in truth without a
    peer.

www.ingramcontent.com/pod-product-compliance
Lightning Source LLC
Chambersburg PA
CBHW022002100426
42738CB00042B/1368